SUPER EASY RECIPES

Publications International, Ltd.

Some of the products listed in this publication may be in limited distribution.

Pictured on the front cover: French Dip Sandwiches *(page 70)* and Greek Pasta Salad *(page 162).*

Pictured on the back cover: Cinnamon Roll-Topped Peach and Raspberry Cobbler *(page 18).*

Photo on cover *(Greek Pasta Salad)* and photo on page 163 © Shutterstock.com.

ISBN: 978-1-64558-743-9

Manufactured in China.

8 7 6 5 4 3 2 1

Microwave Cooking: Microwave ovens vary in wattage. Use the cooking times as guidelines and check for doneness before adding more time.

WARNING: Food preparation, baking and cooking involve inherent dangers: misuse of electric products, sharp electric tools, boiling water, hot stoves, allergic reactions, foodborne illnesses and the like, pose numerous potential risks. Publications International, Ltd. (PIL) assumes no responsibility or liability for any damages you may experience as a result of following recipes, instructions, tips or advice in this publication.

While we hope this publication helps you find new ways to eat delicious foods, you may not always achieve the results desired due to variations in ingredients, cooking temperatures, typos, errors, omissions or individual cooking abilities.

Let's get social!
 @Publications_International
 @PublicationsInternational
www.pilbooks.com

WILD RICE SOUP (PAGE 41)

SAUSAGE AND CHEESE PIZZA (PAGE 94)

CONTENTS

NO-FUSS
BREAKFASTS

QUICK BREAKFAST SANDWICH
MAKES 2 SANDWICHES

2 turkey breakfast sausage patties

3 eggs
Salt and black pepper

2 teaspoons butter

2 slices (about 2 ounces) Cheddar cheese

2 whole wheat English muffins, split and toasted

1 Cook sausage according to package directions; keep warm.

2 Beat eggs, salt and pepper in small bowl. Melt butter in small skillet over low heat. Pour eggs into skillet; cook and stir just until set.

3 Place cheese on bottom halves of English muffins; top with sausage, scrambled eggs and top halves of English muffins. Serve immediately.

TIP
Turkey sausage breakfast patties may vary in size. If patties are small, use two patties for each sandwich.

BREAKFAST FLATS
MAKES 4 SERVINGS

8 slices bacon, chopped

1 package (about 14 ounces) refrigerated pizza dough

All-purpose flour, for dusting

1½ cups (6 ounces) shredded Cheddar cheese

4 eggs

Kosher salt and black pepper (optional)

1 Preheat oven to 400°F. Line two baking sheets with parchment paper.

2 Cook bacon in large nonstick skillet over medium-high heat about 8 minutes or until crisp, stirring occasionally. Remove to paper towel-lined plate to drain.

3 Divide pizza dough into four equal pieces. Roll out each piece into 8½×4-inch rectangle on lightly floured surface; round corners slightly. Place dough on prepared baking sheets; top with cheese and bacon.

4 Bake 10 minutes or until crust is golden brown and crisp and cheese is melted.

5 Meanwhile, spray large skillet with nonstick cooking spray; heat over medium heat. Cook eggs sunny-side up. Top baked flats with fried eggs; season with salt and pepper, if desired. Serve immediately.

QUICK JELLY-FILLED BISCUIT DOUGHNUTS
MAKES 10 DOUGHNUTS

Vegetable oil for frying

1 can (about 7 ounces) refrigerated biscuit dough (10 biscuits)

⅓ cup coarse sugar

1 cup strawberry preserves*

If preserves are very chunky, process in food processor 10 seconds or press through fine-mesh sieve.

1 Pour about 2 inches of oil into Dutch oven or large heavy saucepan; clip deep-fry or candy thermometer to side of Dutch oven. Heat over medium-high heat to 360° to 370°F.

2 Separate biscuits. Place sugar in medium bowl. Fry biscuits in batches 1 minute per side or until puffed and golden. Remove to wire rack. Immediately toss in sugar to coat.

3 Fit piping bag with medium star tip; fill bag with preserves. Poke hole in side of each doughnut with paring knife; fill with preserves. Serve immediately.

CRUSTLESS SPINACH QUICHE

MAKES 6 SERVINGS

8 eggs
1 cup half-and-half
1 teaspoon Italian seasoning
¾ teaspoon salt
½ teaspoon black pepper

1 package (10 ounces) frozen chopped spinach, thawed and squeezed dry
1¼ cups (5 ounces) shredded Italian cheese blend

1 Preheat oven to 350°F. Spray 8-inch round baking pan with nonstick cooking spray.

2 Beat eggs, half-and-half, Italian seasoning, salt and pepper in medium bowl until well blended. Stir in spinach and cheese; mix well. Pour into prepared pan.

3 Bake 33 minutes or until toothpick inserted into center comes out clean. Remove to wire rack; cool 10 minutes before serving.

4 To remove quiche from pan, run knife around edge of pan to loosen. Invert quiche onto plate; invert again onto second plate. Cut into wedges to serve.

BISCUIT-WRAPPED SAUSAGES
MAKES 6 SERVINGS

1 package (8 ounces) refrigerated crescent dough sheet

1 package (about 12 ounces) fully cooked breakfast sausage links

Maple syrup (optional)

1 Unroll crescent dough; cut dough into thin strips. Wrap each sausage with dough. Skewer sausages onto long metal or wooden skewers.* Place on baking sheet.

2 Preheat oven to 350°F.

3 Bake 8 to 10 minutes, turning once, until golden brown.

4 Remove from oven. Cool slightly; remove to serving platter. Serve with maple syrup for dipping, if desired.

*If using wooden skewers, soak in cold water 20 to 30 minutes to prevent burning.

HAM AND EGG BREAKFAST PANINI
MAKES 2 SANDWICHES

¼ cup chopped green or red bell pepper

2 tablespoons sliced green onion

1 slice (1 ounce) reduced-fat smoked deli ham, chopped

½ cup cholesterol-free egg substitute

Black pepper

4 slices multigrain or whole grain bread

2 slices (¾ ounce each) reduced-fat Cheddar or Swiss cheese

1 Spray small nonstick skillet with nonstick cooking spray; heat over medium heat. Add bell pepper and green onion; cook and stir 4 minutes or until crisp-tender. Stir in ham.

2 Whisk egg substitute and black pepper in small bowl until well blended. Pour egg mixture into skillet; cook 2 minutes or until egg mixture is almost set, stirring occasionally.

3 Heat grill pan or medium skillet over medium heat. Spray one side of each bread slice with cooking spray; turn bread over. Top 2 bread slices with 1 cheese slice and half of egg mixture. Top with remaining bread slices.

4 Grill 2 minutes per side, pressing down lightly with spatula until toasted. (Cover pan with lid during last 2 minutes of cooking to melt cheese, if desired.) Serve immediately.

RASPBERRY WHITE CHOCOLATE DANISH
MAKES 8 SERVINGS

1 package (8 ounces) refrigerated crescent roll dough

8 teaspoons red raspberry preserves

1 ounce white baking chocolate, chopped

1 Preheat oven to 375°F. Line large baking sheet with parchment paper or spray with nonstick cooking spray.

2 Unroll crescent dough; separate into eight triangles. Place 1 teaspoon preserves in center of each triangle. Fold right and left corners of long side over filling to top corner to form rectangle. Pinch edges to seal. Place seam side up on prepared baking sheet.

3 Bake 12 minutes or until lightly browned. Remove to wire rack to cool 5 minutes.

4 Place white chocolate in small resealable food storage bag. Microwave on MEDIUM (50%) 1 minute; gently knead bag. Microwave and knead at additional 30-second intervals until chocolate is completely melted. Cut off small corner of bag; drizzle chocolate over danish.

CINNAMON ROLL–TOPPED PEACH AND RASPBERRY COBBLER

MAKES 8 SERVINGS

1 package (16 ounces) frozen peaches, thawed and drained

1 package (12 ounces) frozen raspberries, thawed and drained

½ cup sugar

¼ cup quick-cooking tapioca

¼ cup water

2 teaspoons vanilla

1 teaspoon salt

1 package (about 12 ounces) refrigerated cinnamon rolls with icing

1 Preheat oven to 350°F. Combine peaches, raspberries, sugar, tapioca, water, vanilla and salt in large overproof skillet; stir to blend. Top with cinnamon rolls.

2 Bake 40 to 45 minutes or until golden brown. Drizzle with icing; serve warm.

PARTY STARTERS & SNACKS

PEPPERONI PIZZA DIPPERS
MAKES 4 SERVINGS

1 can (8 ounces) refrigerated crescent dough, without seams preferred

2 tablespoons marinara sauce, plus additional for dipping

4 tablespoons shredded mozzarella cheese

8 slices pepperoni

1 Preheat waffle maker to medium. Carefully unroll dough on cutting board; cut into four rectangles.

2 Place one rectangle of dough on waffle maker; spread with 1 tablespoon sauce, leaving ½-inch border around edges. Top with 1 tablespoon cheese, 4 slices pepperoni, another 1 tablespoon cheese and second rectangle of dough. Close waffle maker.

3 Cook about 8 minutes or until dough is cooked through and golden brown. Repeat with remaining dough, sauce, cheese and pepperoni. Serve warm with additional sauce.

TWISTED CINNAMON STICKS
MAKES 8 SERVINGS

1 cup granulated sugar

3 tablespoons ground cinnamon

1 can (8 ounces) refrigerated crescent roll dough

½ cup (1 stick) butter, melted

....

1 Combine sugar and cinnamon in small bowl; stir to blend. Set aside. Roll each section of dough into long strip; twist around long metal or wooden skewers.* Place on baking sheet.

2 Preheat oven to 350°F.

3 Bake 8 to 10 minutes or until golden brown.

4 Remove from oven. Cool slightly; remove to serving plate. Brush with melted butter and sprinkle with cinnamon-sugar mixture.

*If using wooden skewers, soak in cold water 20 to 30 minutes to prevent burning.

MINI CHEESE DOGS
MAKES 32 MINI CHEESE DOGS

1 package (16 ounces) hot dogs
   (8 hot dogs)
6 ounces pasteurized process
   cheese product

2 packages (16 ounces each)
   jumbo homestyle buttermilk
   biscuits (8 biscuits per
   package)

....

1 Preheat oven to 350°F. Line baking sheet with parchment paper or spray with nonstick cooking spray.

2 Cut each hot dog into four pieces. Cut cheese product into 32 (1×½-inch) pieces.

3 Separate biscuits; cut each biscuit in half. Wrap dough around 1 piece of hot dog and 1 piece of cheese. Place seam side up on baking sheet.

4 Bake 15 minutes or until biscuits are golden brown. Serve warm.

....

VEGGIE VARIATION

To make this snack vegetarian-friendly, substitute 8 veggie dogs (soy protein links) for the regular hot dogs. Veggie dogs can be found in the produce section and sometimes the freezer section of the supermarket.

PEPPERONI BREAD
MAKES ABOUT 6 SERVINGS

1 package (about 14 ounces) refrigerated pizza dough

8 slices provolone cheese

20 to 30 slices pepperoni (about half of 6-ounce package)

½ teaspoon Italian seasoning

¾ cup (3 ounces) shredded mozzarella cheese

½ cup grated Parmesan cheese

1 egg, beaten

Marinara sauce, heated

1 Preheat oven to 400°F. Unroll pizza dough on sheet of parchment paper with long side in front of you. Cut off corners of dough to create oval shape.

2 Arrange half of provolone slices over bottom half of oval, cutting to fit as necessary. Top with pepperoni; sprinkle with ¼ teaspoon Italian seasoning. Top with mozzarella, Parmesan cheese and remaining provolone slices; sprinkle with remaining ¼ teaspoon Italian seasoning.

3 Fold top half of dough over filling to create half moon (calzone) shape; press edges with fork or pinch edges to seal. Transfer calzone with parchment paper to large baking sheet; curve slightly into crescent shape. Brush with beaten egg.

4 Bake about 16 minutes or until crust is golden brown. Remove to wire rack to cool slightly. Cut crosswise into slices; serve warm with marinara sauce.

FRENCH-STYLE PIZZA BITES
MAKES ABOUT 24 SERVINGS

2 tablespoons olive oil

1 medium onion, thinly sliced

1 medium red bell pepper, cut into 3-inch-long strips

2 cloves garlic, minced

⅓ cup pitted black olives, cut into thin wedges

1 package (about 14 ounces) refrigerated pizza dough

¾ cup (3 ounces) finely shredded Swiss or Gruyère cheese

1 Position oven rack to lowest position. Preheat oven to 425°F. Grease large baking sheet.

2 Heat oil in medium skillet over medium heat. Add onion, bell pepper and garlic. Cook and stir 5 minutes or until crisp-tender. Stir in olives. Remove from heat; set aside.

3 Pat dough into 16×12-inch rectangle on prepared baking sheet. Arrange onion mixture over dough; sprinkle with cheese. Bake 10 minutes. Loosen crust with long spatula; slide onto oven rack. Bake 3 to 5 minutes more or until golden brown.

4 Slide baking sheet under crust and remove crust from rack. Transfer to cutting board. Cut pizza crosswise into eight 1¾-inch-wide strips; cut diagonally into ten 2-inch-wide strips, making diamond pieces. Serve immediately.

SWEET & SOUR SHRIMP SKEWERS
MAKES 10 TO 12 SERVINGS

½ pound medium raw shrimp, peeled and deveined (with tails on)

1 can (8 ounces) pineapple chunks in juice, drained

¼ cup sweet and sour sauce

1 Alternately thread shrimp and pineapple chunks onto wooden skewers. Brush with sweet and sour sauce.

2 Heat large nonstick grill pan over medium-high heat. Cook skewers 3 minutes on each side or until shrimp are pink and opaque. Serve with additional sweet and sour sauce for dipping, if desired.

CHEESE AND CHUTNEY CUPS
MAKES 15 APPETIZERS

1 package frozen mini phyllo cups (15 cups)

1 cup garlic and herb spreadable cheese

3 tablespoons mango chutney

1 Defrost phyllo shells according to package directions.

2 Spoon or pipe about 1 tablespoon cheese into each cup. Top with about ½ teaspoon chutney.

VARIATION
Try topping these tarts with drained chopped roasted red peppers instead of the chutney.

APRICOT BRIE EN CROÛTE
MAKES 6 SERVINGS

1 sheet frozen puff pastry (half of 17¼-ounce package)

1 round Brie cheese (8 ounces)
¼ cup apricot preserves

1 Unfold puff pastry; thaw 20 minutes on lightly floured surface. Preheat oven to 400°F. Line baking sheet with parchment paper.

2 Roll out puff pastry to 12-inch square. Place cheese in center of square; spread preserves over top of cheese.

3 Gather up edges of puff pastry; bring together over center of cheese, covering entirely. Pinch and twist pastry edges together to seal. Transfer to prepared baking sheet.

4 Bake 20 to 25 minutes or until golden brown. (If top of pastry browns too quickly, cover loosely with small piece of foil.) Serve warm.

VARIATION

For added flavor and texture, sprinkle 2 tablespoons sliced almonds over the preserves. Proceed with wrapping and baking the Brie as directed.

BACON-WRAPPED TERIYAKI SHRIMP
MAKES 4 TO 5 SERVINGS

1 pound large raw shrimp, peeled and deveined (with tails on)

¼ cup teriyaki marinade

11 to 12 slices bacon, cut in half crosswise

1 Preheat oven to 425°F. Line shallow baking pan with foil.

2 Place shrimp in large resealable food storage bag. Add teriyaki marinade; seal bag and turn to coat. Marinate in refrigerator 15 to 20 minutes.

3 Remove shrimp from bag; reserve marinade. Wrap each shrimp with 1 piece bacon. Place shrimp in prepared baking pan; brush bacon with some of reserved marinade.

4 Bake 15 minutes or until bacon is crisp and shrimp are pink and opaque.

TIP
Do not use thick-cut bacon for this recipe, because the bacon will not be completely cooked when the shrimp are cooked through.

SPEEDY SALAMI SPIRALS
MAKES ABOUT 28 SPIRALS

1 package (about 14 ounces) refrigerated pizza dough

1 cup (4 ounces) shredded Italian cheese blend

3 to 4 ounces thinly sliced Genoa salami

....

1 Preheat oven to 400°F. Line large baking sheet with parchment paper or spray with nonstick cooking spray.

2 Unroll dough on cutting board or clean work surface; press into 15×10-inch rectangle. Sprinkle evenly with cheese; top with salami.

3 Starting with long side, tightly roll up dough and filling jelly-roll style, pinching seam to seal. Cut roll crosswise into ½-inch slices; place slices cut sides up on prepared baking sheet. (If roll is too soft to cut, refrigerate or freeze until firm.)

4 Bake about 15 minutes or until golden brown. Serve warm.

PESTO SCALLOP SKEWERS
MAKES 16 APPETIZERS

1 to 2 red or yellow bell peppers, cut into bite-size pieces

16 jumbo sea scallops (about 1 pound)

2 tablespoons prepared pesto

....

1 Thread two bell pepper pieces and one scallop onto each of 16 short wooden skewers. Brush pesto over bell peppers and scallops.

2 Heat nonstick grill pan or large nonstick skillet over medium-high heat. Cook skewers 2 to 3 minutes on each side or until scallops are opaque in center.

....

CHOCOLATE ALMOND CHERRY SNACK MIX
MAKES 6 CUPS

2 cups whole blanched almonds*

2 cups red and green candy-coated chocolate pieces

2 cups dried cherries

For more flavor, toast almonds; spread in single layer in heavy-bottomed skillet. Cook over medium heat 1 to 2 minutes, stirring frequently, until lightly browned. Remove from skillet immediately. Cool before using.

....

Combine all ingredients in medium serving bowl; mix well. Store leftovers in an airtight container.

PESTO SCALLOP SKEWERS

SUPER SOUPS & STEWS

WILD RICE SOUP
MAKES 6 SERVINGS

½ cup dried lentils, rinsed and sorted

1 package (6 ounces) long grain and wild rice blend

1 can (about 14 ounces) vegetable broth

1 bag (10 ounces) frozen mixed vegetables

1 cup milk

2 slices (1 ounce each) American cheese, cut into pieces

1 Place lentils in small saucepan; cover with about 3 cups water. Bring to a boil over medium-high heat. Reduce heat to low. Simmer, covered, 5 minutes. Let stand, covered, 1 hour. Drain and rinse lentils.

2 Cook rice according to package directions. Add lentils, broth, mixed vegetables, milk and cheese. Bring to a boil over medium-high heat. Reduce heat to low. Simmer, uncovered, 20 minutes.

CHICKEN TORTELLINI SOUP

MAKES 4 SERVINGS

6 cups chicken broth

1 package (9 ounces) refrigerated cheese and spinach tortellini

1 package (about 6 ounces) refrigerated fully cooked chicken breast strips, cut into bite-size pieces

2 cups baby spinach

4 to 6 tablespoons grated Parmesan cheese

1 tablespoon chopped fresh chives *or* 2 tablespoons sliced green onion

1 Bring broth to a boil in large saucepan over high heat; add tortellini. Reduce heat to medium; cook 5 minutes. Stir in chicken and spinach.

2 Reduce heat to low; cook 3 minutes or until chicken is heated through. Sprinkle with Parmesan cheese and chives.

BLACK AND WHITE CHILI
MAKES 6 SERVINGS

1 pound chicken tenders, cut into ¾-inch pieces

1 cup coarsely chopped onion

1 can (about 15 ounces) Great Northern beans, drained

1 can (about 15 ounces) black beans, drained

1 can (about 14 ounces) Mexican-style stewed tomatoes, undrained

2 tablespoons Texas-style chili powder seasoning mix

....

SLOW COOKER DIRECTIONS

1 Spray large skillet with nonstick cooking spray; heat over medium heat until hot. Add chicken and onion; cook and stir 5 minutes or until chicken is browned.

2 Combine chicken mixture, beans, tomatoes with juice and chili seasoning in slow cooker. Cover; cook on LOW 4 to 4½ hours.

....

SERVING SUGGESTION

For a change of pace, this delicious chili is excellent served over cooked rice or pasta.

MUSHROOM-BEEF STEW

MAKES 4 SERVINGS

1 pound beef stew meat

1 can (10¾ ounces) condensed cream of mushroom soup, undiluted

2 cans (4 ounces each) sliced mushrooms, drained

1 package (1 ounce) dry onion soup mix

Hot cooked noodles

SLOW COOKER DIRECTIONS

1 Combine beef, condensed soup, mushrooms and dry soup mix in slow cooker. Cover; cook on LOW 8 to 10 hours.

2 Serve over noodles.

SWISS STEAK STEW

MAKES 10 SERVINGS

2 to 3 boneless beef top sirloin steaks (about 4 pounds)

2 cans (about 14 ounces each) diced tomatoes

2 medium green bell peppers, cut into ½-inch strips

2 medium onions, coarsely chopped

1 tablespoon seasoned salt

1 teaspoon black pepper

SLOW COOKER DIRECTIONS

Cut each steak into 3 to 4 pieces; place in slow cooker. Add tomatoes, bell peppers and onions. Sprinkle with seasoned salt and black pepper. Cover; cook on LOW 8 hours or until beef is tender.

TIP

To increase the flavor of the finished dish and more closely follow the traditional preparation of Swiss steak, dust the steak pieces with flour and brown in a bit of olive oil in a large skillet over medium-high heat before adding them to the slow cooker.

EGG DROP SOUP
MAKES 2 SERVINGS

2 cans (about 14 ounces each) chicken broth

1 tablespoon soy sauce

2 teaspoons cornstarch

½ cup cholesterol-free egg substitute

¼ cup thinly sliced green onions

1 Bring broth to a boil in large saucepan over high heat. Reduce heat to medium-low.

2 Stir soy sauce and cornstarch in small bowl until smooth and well blended; stir into broth. Cook and stir 2 minutes or until slightly thickened.

3 Stirring constantly in one direction, slowly pour egg substitute in thin stream into soup.

4 Ladle soup into bowls; sprinkle with green onions.

QUICK & EASY MEATBALL SOUP
MAKES 4 TO 6 SERVINGS

1 package (15 to 18 ounces) frozen Italian sausage meatballs without sauce

2 cans (about 14 ounces each) Italian-style stewed tomatoes

2 cans (about 14 ounces each) beef broth

1 can (about 14 ounces) mixed vegetables

½ cup uncooked rotini pasta or small macaroni

½ teaspoon dried oregano

1 Thaw meatballs in microwave according to package directions.

2 Place tomatoes, broth, mixed vegetables, pasta and oregano in large saucepan. Add meatballs; bring to a boil over medium-high heat. Reduce heat to medium-low. Simmer, covered, 15 minutes or until pasta is tender.

MINESTRONE SOUP
MAKES 4 TO 6 SERVINGS

¾ cup uncooked small shell pasta

2 cans (about 14 ounces each) vegetable broth

1 can (28 ounces) crushed tomatoes in tomato purée

1 can (about 15 ounces) white beans, rinsed and drained

1 package (16 ounces) frozen vegetable medley, such as broccoli, green beans, carrots and red peppers

4 to 6 teaspoons prepared pesto

1 Cook pasta according to package directions; drain.

2 Meanwhile, combine broth, tomatoes and beans in large saucepan; bring to a boil over high heat. Reduce heat to low; cover and simmer 3 to 5 minutes.

3 Add vegetables to broth mixture; return to a boil over high heat. Stir in pasta; simmer, uncovered, until vegetables are tender. Ladle soup into bowls; Top each serving with about 1 teaspoon pesto.

ALL-IN-ONE BURGER STEW

MAKES 6 SERVINGS

1 pound lean ground beef

2 cups frozen Italian-style vegetables

1 can (about 14 ounces) diced tomatoes with basil and garlic

1 can (about 14 ounces) beef broth

2½ cups uncooked medium egg noodles

Salt and black pepper

....

1 Brown beef in Dutch oven or large skillet over medium-high heat 6 to 8 minutes, stirring to break up meat. Drain fat.

2 Add vegetables, tomatoes and broth; bring to a boil over high heat.

3 Stir in noodles. Reduce heat to medium; cover and cook 12 to 15 minutes or until vegetables and noodles are tender. Season with salt and pepper.

....

NOTE

For a special touch, sprinkle with chopped parsley before serving.

....

TIP

To complete this meal, serve with breadsticks or a loaf of Italian bread and a simple salad.

POTATO-BACON SOUP
MAKES 4 SERVINGS

2 cans (about 14 ounces each) chicken broth

3 russet potatoes (1¾ to 2 pounds), peeled and cut into ½-inch cubes

1 medium onion, finely chopped

1 teaspoon dried thyme

4 to 6 slices bacon (4 to 6 ounces), chopped

½ cup (2 ounces) shredded Cheddar cheese

1 Combine broth, potatoes, onion and thyme in Dutch oven; bring to a boil over high heat. Reduce heat to medium-high and boil 10 minutes or until potatoes are tender.

2 While potatoes are cooking, place bacon on microwavable plate. Cover with paper towels; cook at HIGH 6 to 7 minutes or until bacon is crisp, stirring after 3 minutes.

3 Immediately add bacon to broth mixture; simmer 3 to 5 minutes. Season to taste with salt and pepper. Ladle into bowls and sprinkle with cheese.

NOTE

Instead of using a knife to chop the bacon, try snipping it with a pair of scissors while it is partially frozen—you'll find this method quicker and easier.

SATISFYING
SANDWICHES & WRAPS

LETTUCE-WRAPPED TURKEY CLUB
MAKES 2 SERVINGS

8 large romaine lettuce leaves

8 thin slices deli-style turkey breast (about 4 ounces total)

2 medium tomatoes, cut into 8 slices each

2 tablespoons real bacon bits

¼ cup ranch salad dressing

Black pepper (optional)

. . . .

Layer lettuce, turkey, tomato and bacon bits on two plates. Drizzle with dressing. Season with pepper, if desired.

. . . .

VARIATION
Layer Lettuce-Wrapped Turkey Club on large tortilla or between 2 slices of bread, if you prefer.

PARMESAN SLIDERS

MAKES 10 TO 12 APPETIZERS

¾ to 1 cup freshly shredded
   Parmesan cheese

⅓ cup milk

1¼ teaspoons chili powder

½ teaspoon sugar

1 cup biscuit baking mix

1 tablespoon cold unsalted
   butter, cut into thin slices

Dijon-style mustard

Thinly sliced prosciutto, deli
   pastrami or ham

1 Preheat oven to 400°F. Line baking sheet with parchment paper or coat with nonstick cooking spray; set aside. Spread cheese on large plate; set aside. Combine milk, chili powder and sugar in small bowl. Stir well; set aside 5 minutes.

2 Place biscuit mix in medium bowl. Cut in butter with pastry blender or two knives until mixture resembles coarse crumbs. Add milk mixture; stir gently to form soft sticky dough. Drop dough by rounded tablespoonfuls onto cheese; gently roll dough to coat all sides with cheese. Place on prepared baking sheet.

3 Bake 13 to 14 minutes or until biscuits are golden. Transfer biscuits to wire rack to cool slightly. To serve, split each biscuit. Spread mustard on bottom half. Evenly divide prosciutto among biscuits and top with remaining halves.

GRILLED BUFFALO CHICKEN WRAPS
MAKES 4 SERVINGS

4 boneless skinless chicken breasts (about 4 ounces each)

¼ cup plus 2 tablespoons buffalo wing sauce, divided

2 cups broccoli slaw

1 tablespoon light blue cheese salad dressing

4 (8-inch) whole wheat tortillas, warmed

1 Place chicken in large resealable food storage bag. Add ¼ cup buffalo sauce; seal bag. Marinate in refrigerator 15 minutes.

2 Meanwhile, prepare grill for direct cooking over medium-high heat. Grill chicken 5 to 6 minutes per side or until no longer pink. When cool enough to handle, slice chicken and combine with remaining 2 tablespoons buffalo sauce in medium bowl.

3 Combine broccoli slaw and blue cheese dressing in medium bowl; mix well.

4 Arrange chicken and broccoli slaw evenly down center of each tortilla. Roll up to secure filling. To serve, cut in half diagonally.

TIPS

If you don't like the spicy flavor of buffalo wing sauce, substitute your favorite barbecue sauce.

For quicker preparation, start with cooked chicken strips topped with buffalo wing sauce, then follow directions starting with Step 3.

BARBECUE BEEF SANDWICHES

MAKES 4 SERVINGS

2½ pounds boneless beef chuck roast

2 tablespoons Southwest seasoning

1 tablespoon vegetable oil

1¼ cups beef broth

2½ cups barbecue sauce, divided

4 sandwich or pretzel buns, split

1⅓ cups prepared coleslaw* (preferably vinegar based)

Vinegar-based coleslaws provide a perfect complement to the rich beef; they can often be found at the salad bar or prepared foods section of large supermarkets.

1 Sprinkle both sides of beef with Southwest seasoning. Heat oil in Dutch oven over medium-high heat. Add beef; cook about 6 minutes per side or until browned. Remove to plate.

2 Add broth; cook 2 minutes, scraping up browned bits from bottom of Dutch oven. Stir in 2 cups barbecue sauce; bring to a boil. Return beef to Dutch oven; turn to coat.

3 Reduce heat to low; cover and cook 3 to 3½ hours or until beef is fork-tender, turning beef halfway through cooking time.

4 Remove beef to large plate; let stand until cool enough to handle. Meanwhile, cook sauce remaining in Dutch oven over high heat about 10 minutes or until reduced and slightly thickened.

5 Shred beef into bite-size pieces. Stir in 1 cup reduced cooking sauce and ¼ cup barbecue sauce. Add remaining ¼ cup barbecue sauce, if desired. Fill buns with beef mixture; top with coleslaw.

NOTE

To shred beef, face two forks back to back, pull forks in opposite directions breaking up meat as you pull.

CHORIZO QUESADILLAS
MAKES 6 SERVINGS

1 package (9 ounces) chorizo

1 cup coarsely chopped cauliflower

1 small onion, finely chopped

12 (6-inch) flour tortillas

1½ cups (6 ounces) chihuahua cheese

6 teaspoons vegetable oil

Salsa, guacamole and sour cream

1 Heat medium skillet over medium-high heat. Add chorizo, cauliflower and onion; cook and stir 10 to 12 minutes or until cauliflower is tender. Transfer to bowl. Wipe out skillet.

2 Spread ¼ cup chorizo mixture onto each of six tortillas. Top with ¼ cup cheese and remaining tortillas.

3 Heat 1 teaspoon oil in same skillet over medium-high heat. Add one quesadilla; cook 2 to 3 minutes per side or until well browned and cheese is melted. Repeat with remaining oil and quesadillas. Cut into wedges; serve with salsa, guacamole and sour cream.

NOTE

To keep cooked quesadillas warm, arrange on a baking sheet and place in a preheated 200°F oven until all the quesadillas are cooked and ready to serve.

FRENCH DIP SANDWICHES
MAKES 6 SERVINGS

3 pounds boneless beef chuck roast

½ teaspoon salt

½ teaspoon black pepper

1 tablespoon olive oil

2 large onions, cut into halves, then cut into ¼-inch slices

2¼ cups reduced-sodium beef broth, divided

3 tablespoons Worcestershire sauce

6 hoagie rolls, split and heated

12 slices provolone cheese

1 Season beef with salt and pepper. Heat oil in Dutch oven or large saucepan over medium-high heat. Add beef; cook about 6 minutes per side or until browned. Remove to plate.

2 Add onions and ¼ cup broth to Dutch oven; cook 8 minutes or until golden brown, stirring occasionally and scraping up browned bits from bottom of pot. Remove half of onions to small bowl; set aside. Stir remaining 2 cups broth and Worcestershire sauce in Dutch oven; mix well. Return beef to Dutch oven. Reduce heat to low; cover and cook 3 to 3½ hours or until beef is fork-tender.

3 Remove beef to large bowl; let stand until cool enough to handle. Shred into bite-size pieces. Add ⅔ cup cooking liquid; toss to coat. Pour remaining cooking liquid into small bowl for serving.

4 Top bottom halves of rolls with cheese, beef and reserved onions. Serve with warm au jus for dipping.

NOTE

To shred beef, face two forks back to back, pull forks in opposite directions breaking up meat as you pull.

BIRCH BARK SANDWICH
MAKES 1 SERVING

1 (10-inch) flour tortilla

1 tablespoon mayonnaise

1 teaspoon mustard

4 slices (about 6×4-inch) deli ham

1 teaspoon whipped cream cheese

½ cup alfalfa, clover or radish sprouts

....

1 Spread one side of tortilla with mayonnaise and mustard. Lay ham slices on tortilla. Tightly roll tortilla, forming a log.

2 Serve on alfalfa sprouts.

....

NOTE

Recipe is easily scaled up to prepare enough for any serving size. Feel free to substitute any preferred deli meat for ham.

QUICK CHICKEN QUESADILLAS
MAKES 4 SERVINGS

4 boneless skinless chicken breasts

3 tablespoons vegetable oil, divided

½ teaspoon salt

1 large yellow onion, thinly sliced

8 (6- to 8-inch) flour tortillas

3 cups (12 ounces) shredded mild Cheddar or Monterey Jack cheese

Salsa, sour cream and/or guacamole (optional)

1 Cut chicken into 1×¼-inch strips.

2 Heat 2 tablespoons oil in large skillet over high heat. Add chicken; cook 3 to 4 minutes or until lightly browned and cooked through, stirring occasionally. Season with salt. Remove to plate.

3 Add onion to skillet; cook and stir about 5 minutes or until translucent. Remove to plate.

4 Heat remaining 1 tablespoon oil in same skillet. Place 1 tortilla in skillet; top with one quarter each of chicken, onion and cheese. Place second tortilla over filling; press down lightly. Cook quesadilla about 2 minutes per side or until browned and crisp. Repeat with remaining tortillas and filling.

5 Cut into wedges; serve with desired toppings.

NOTE
Be creative and use your own favorite fillings!

DELI BEEF WRAPS WITH CREAMY HONEY-MUSTARD SPREAD
MAKES 4 WRAPS

3 tablespoons light mayonnaise

1 tablespoon honey mustard

1½ teaspoons packed dark brown sugar (optional)

4 whole grain or whole wheat tortillas

2 cups packed shredded lettuce

6 ounces thinly sliced deli roast beef

1 medium green bell pepper, thinly sliced

¼ cup thinly sliced red onion

1 Stir mayonnaise, honey mustard and brown sugar, if desired, in small bowl until well blended. Spread evenly on tortillas.

2 Layer lettuce, roast beef, bell pepper and onion evenly on tortillas. Roll up to enclose filling. Serve immediately or refrigerate up to 6 hours.

VARIATION

Stir chopped fresh cilantro into the mayonnaise mixture and add a layer of chopped avocado.

TIC-TAC-TOE SANDWICH

MAKES 1 SANDWICH

2 teaspoons mayonnaise

1 slice whole wheat sandwich bread

1 slice white sandwich bread

1 slice (1 ounce) cheese

1 slice deli ham

3 green or black olives

1 Spread 1 teaspoon mayonnaise on each bread slice. Layer cheese and ham on 1 bread slice. Top with remaining bread slice.

2 Trim crust from sandwich. Cut sandwich into nine squares by cutting into thirds in each direction. Turn alternating pieces over to form checkerboard pattern.

3 Thinly slice 1 olive to form 'O's. Cut remaining 2 olives into strips. Place olive pieces on sandwich squares to form 'X's and 'O's.

CHICKEN, HUMMUS AND VEGETABLE WRAPS

MAKES 4 SERVINGS

¾ cup hummus (regular, roasted red pepper or roasted garlic)

4 (8- to 10-inch) sun-dried tomato or spinach wraps *or* whole wheat tortillas

2 cups chopped cooked chicken breast

Chipotle hot pepper sauce or Louisiana-style hot pepper sauce (optional)

½ cup shredded carrots

½ cup chopped unpeeled cucumber

½ cup thinly sliced radishes

2 tablespoons chopped fresh mint *or* basil

Spread hummus evenly over wraps all the way to edges. Arrange chicken over hummus; sprinkle with hot pepper sauce, if desired. Top with carrots, cucumber, radishes and mint. Roll up tightly. Cut in half diagonally.

VARIATION

Substitute alfalfa sprouts for the radishes. For tasty appetizers, cut wraps into bite-size pieces.

EASY FAMILY BURRITOS
MAKES 8 SERVINGS

1 boneless beef chuck shoulder
     roast (2 to 3 pounds)

1 jar (24 ounces) *or* 2 jars
     (16 ounces each) salsa
   Flour tortillas, warmed

SLOW COOKER DIRECTIONS

1 Place roast in slow cooker; top with salsa. Cover; cook on LOW 8 to 10 hours.

2 Remove beef from slow cooker. Shred beef with two forks. Return to slow cooker. Cover; cook 1 to 2 hours or until heated through.

3 Serve shredded beef wrapped in warm tortillas.

SERVING SUGGESTION

Serve these tasty burritos with any combination
of toppings, such as shredded cheese, sour cream,
salsa, lettuce, tomato, onion or guacamole.

TIP

Make a batch of burrito meat and freeze it in family-size
portions. It's quick and easy to reheat in the microwave
on busy nights when there's no time to cook.

FAVORITE FLATBREADS & PIZZA

CHICKEN PESTO FLATBREADS
MAKES 2 SERVINGS

2 (6- to 7-inch) round flatbreads or Greek-style pita bread rounds (no pocket)

2 tablespoons prepared pesto sauce

1 cup grilled chicken strips

4 slices (1 ounce each) mozzarella cheese

1 plum tomato, cut into ¼-inch slices

3 tablespoons shredded Parmesan cheese

1 Place flatbreads on work surface. Spread 1 tablespoon pesto over half of each flatbread. Place chicken on opposite half of bread; top with mozzarella, tomato and Parmesan cheese. Fold pesto-topped bread half over filling.

2 Spray grill pan or nonstick skillet with nonstick cooking spray or brush with vegetable oil; heat over medium-high heat. Cook sandwiches about 3 minutes per side or until bread is toasted, cheese begins to melt and sandwiches are heated through.

PEPPER PITA PIZZAS
MAKES 4 SERVINGS

1 teaspoon olive oil

1 medium onion, thinly sliced

1 medium red bell pepper, cut into thin strips

1 medium green bell pepper, cut into thin strips

4 cloves garlic, minced

2 tablespoons minced fresh basil *or* 2 teaspoons dried basil

1 tablespoon minced fresh oregano *or* 1 teaspoon dried oregano

2 Italian plum tomatoes, coarsely chopped

4 (6-inch) pita bread rounds

1 cup (4 ounces) shredded reduced-fat Monterey Jack cheese

1 Preheat oven to 425°F. Heat oil in medium nonstick skillet over medium heat until hot. Add onion, bell peppers, garlic, basil and oregano. Cook 5 minutes or until tender, stirring occasionally. Add tomatoes. Cook 3 minutes.

2 Place pita rounds on baking sheet. Divide tomato mixture evenly among pitas; top each pita with ¼ cup cheese. Bake 5 minutes or until cheese is melted.

WILD MUSHROOM FLATBREAD
MAKES 16 PIECES (ABOUT 8 SERVINGS)

1 package (about 14 ounces) refrigerated pizza dough

2 teaspoons olive oil

1 package (4 ounces) sliced cremini mushrooms

1 package (4 ounces) sliced shiitake mushrooms

1 shallot, thinly sliced

2 cloves garlic, minced

½ teaspoon salt

¾ cup (3 ounces) grated Gruyère cheese

2 teaspoons chopped fresh thyme

1 Preheat oven to 400°F. Line baking sheet with parchment paper. Spray with nonstick cooking spray.

2 Roll out pizza dough on lightly floured surface to 15×10-inch rectangle. Place on prepared baking sheet. Bake 10 minutes.

3 Meanwhile, heat oil in large nonstick skillet over medium-high heat. Add mushrooms; cook and stir 5 minutes. Add shallot and garlic; cook and stir 5 minutes or until tender. Season with salt.

4 Arrange mushroom mixture evenly over prepared pizza crust. Top evenly with cheese and thyme.

5 Bake 8 minutes or until cheese is melted. To serve, cut into 16 pieces.

PEPPERONI PIZZA ROLLS
MAKES 12 ROLLS

1 package (about 14 ounces) refrigerated pizza dough

½ cup pizza sauce, plus additional sauce for serving

⅓ cup chopped pepperoni or mini pepperoni slices (half of 2½-ounce package)

9 to 10 slices (1 ounce each) fontina, provolone or provolone-mozzarella blend cheese*

*For best results, use thinner cheese slices which are less than 1 ounce each.

....

1 Spray 12 standard (2½-inch) muffin pan cups with nonstick cooking spray.

2 Roll out pizza dough on lightly floured surface into 12×9-inch rectangle. Spread ½ cup pizza sauce over dough, leaving ½-inch border on one long side. Sprinkle with pepperoni; top with cheese, cutting cheese slices to fit as necessary. Starting with long side opposite ½-inch border, tightly roll up dough; pinch seam to seal.

3 Cut crosswise into 1-inch slices; place slices cut sides up in prepared muffin cups. Preheat oven to 400°F.

4 Bake 8 to 10 minutes or until golden brown. Loosen bottom and sides with small spatula or knife; remove to wire rack. Serve warm with additional sauce for dipping, if desired.

BBQ CHICKEN FLATBREAD

MAKES 4 SERVINGS

3 tablespoons red wine vinegar

2 teaspoons sugar

¼ red onion, thinly sliced (about ⅓ cup)

3 cups shredded rotisserie chicken

½ cup barbecue sauce

1 package (about 14 ounces) refrigerated pizza dough

All-purpose flour, for dusting

1½ cups (6 ounces) shredded mozzarella cheese

1 green onion, thinly sliced diagonally

2 tablespoons chopped fresh cilantro

··

1 Preheat oven to 400°F. Line baking sheet with parchment paper.

2 For pickled onion, combine vinegar and sugar in small bowl; stir until sugar is dissolved. Add red onion; cover and let stand at room temperature while preparing flatbread. Combine chicken and barbecue sauce in medium bowl; toss to coat.

3 Roll out dough into 11×9-inch rectangle on lightly floured surface. Transfer dough to prepared baking sheet; top with cheese and barbecue chicken mixture.

4 Bake about 12 minutes or until crust is golden brown and cheese is melted. Drain red onion. Sprinkle red onion, green onion and cilantro over flatbread. Serve immediately.

SAUSAGE AND CHEESE PIZZA

MAKES 8 SERVINGS

1 package (about 14 ounces) refrigerated pizza dough

1 medium red onion, thinly sliced

4 ounces cooked turkey sausage breakfast links (5 to 6 links), thinly sliced

1 medium green bell pepper, thinly sliced

¾ cup pizza sauce

Red pepper flakes (optional)

1 cup (4 ounces) shredded low-fat Monterey Jack or pizza cheese blend

1 Preheat oven to 425°F. Spray 15×10-inch jelly-roll pan with nonstick cooking spray. Unroll dough on pan; press to edges of pan. Bake about 6 minutes or until crust begins to brown.

2 Spray large nonstick skillet with cooking spray. Cook and stir onion over medium-high heat until tender. Add sausage and bell pepper to skillet. Cook and stir about 5 minutes or until bell pepper is crisp-tender.

3 Spread pizza sauce evenly over crust; top with sausage mixture. Sprinkle with red pepper flakes, if desired. Top with cheese.

4 Bake 7 to 10 minutes or until crust is golden brown and cheese is melted. Cut pizza into eight pieces to serve.

SPINACH FLORENTINE FLATBREAD
MAKES 8 SERVINGS

1 tablespoon olive oil

2 cloves garlic, minced

1 package (10 ounces) baby spinach

1 can (about 14 ounces) quartered artichoke hearts, drained and sliced

½ teaspoon salt

¼ teaspoon dried oregano

Pinch black pepper

Pinch red pepper flakes

2 rectangular pizza or flatbread crusts (about 8 ounces each)

1 plum tomato, seeded and diced

2 cups (8 ounces) shredded Monterey Jack cheese

½ cup (2 ounces) shredded Italian cheese blend

Shredded fresh basil leaves (optional)

•••••••••••••••••••••••••••••••••••••

1 Preheat oven to 425°F.

2 Heat oil in large skillet over medium-high heat. Add garlic; cook and stir 30 seconds. Add spinach; cook and stir about 3 minutes or until completely wilted, stirring occasionally. Transfer to medium bowl; stir in artichokes, salt and oregano. Season with black pepper and red pepper flakes.

3 Place pizza crusts on large baking sheet. Spread spinach mixture over crusts; sprinkle with tomato, Monterey Jack cheese and Italian cheese blend.

4 Bake 12 minutes or until cheeses are melted and edges of crusts are browned. Garnish with basil.

•••••••••••••••••••••••••••••••••••••

TIP
For crispier crusts, bake flatbreads on a preheated pizza stone or directly on the oven rack.

RAMEN PIZZA PIE

MAKES 6 SERVINGS

2 packages (3 ounces each) ramen noodles, any flavor*

2 eggs, lightly beaten

¼ cup milk

¼ teaspoon salt

1 cup ricotta cheese

1 cup pasta sauce**

1 cup (4 ounces) shredded part-skim mozzarella cheese

Discard seasoning packets.

**For added flavor, choose a tomato-basil flavored sauce.*

•••••••••••••••••••••••••••••••••••••••

1 Preheat oven to 425°F. Grease a 9-inch pie pan. Cook noodles according to package directions; drain well.

2 Whisk eggs, milk and salt in large bowl. Stir in noodles; toss to coat. Spread evenly in bottom of prepared pan. Bake 10 minutes or until set.

3 Top crust with ricotta cheese, pasta sauce and mozzarella cheese. Bake 15 minutes or until cheeses are melted and golden brown. Let stand 5 minutes before serving.

RUSTIC ROASTED RED PEPPER, ROSEMARY AND PANCETTA FLATBREAD

MAKES 6 SERVINGS

1 can (11 ounces) refrigerated thin pizza crust

2 tablespoons sun-dried tomato dressing

1 large yellow onion, thinly sliced

2 ounces pancetta,* chopped

2 cloves garlic, crushed

1 jar (7 ounces) roasted red peppers in water, drained and sliced

1 tablespoon chopped fresh rosemary

¼ cup shredded Parmesan cheese

Pancetta is Italian bacon. Unlike American bacon, which is most often smoked, pancetta is unsmoked pork belly that's cured in salt and spices such as nutmeg, black pepper and fennel. It's then dried for a few months. If you can't find pancetta, you may use 2 ounces of bacon instead.

1 Heat oven to 400°F. Unroll pizza crust on baking sheet sprayed with nonstick cooking spray. Fold edges over to form ½-inch rim. Bake 5 minutes.

2 Place dressing in large nonstick skillet heated over medium heat. Add onion and cook 6 minutes. Add pancetta and garlic; cook an additional 4 minutes. Spread over pizza crust.

3 Layer peppers on pizza. Sprinkle with rosemary and Parmesan cheese. Bake 10 minutes or until cheese melts and crust edges are brown.

NOTE

Be sure to buy roasted red peppers in water and not in oil. Check the ingredient list to be sure.

TIP

Kitchen scissors are a great tool for cutting pizzas and flatbreads—neater and easier to handle than a pizza cutter.

PIZZA ROLLERS
MAKES 6 SERVINGS

1 package (about 14 ounces) refrigerated pizza dough

½ cup pizza sauce

18 slices turkey pepperoni

6 sticks mozzarella cheese

1 Preheat oven to 425°F. Coat baking sheet with nonstick cooking spray.

2 Roll out pizza dough on baking sheet to form 12×9-inch rectangle. Cut pizza dough into six 4½×4-inch rectangles. Spread about 1 tablespoon sauce down center third of each rectangle. Top with 3 slices pepperoni and stick of mozzarella cheese. Bring ends of dough together over cheese, pinching to seal. Place seam side down on prepared baking sheet.

3 Bake in center of oven 10 minutes or until golden brown.

GYPSY'S BBQ CHICKEN
MAKES 6 SERVINGS

6 boneless skinless chicken breasts (about 1½ pounds)

1 bottle (26 ounces) barbecue sauce

6 slices bacon

6 slices (1 ounce each) Swiss cheese

....

SLOW COOKER DIRECTIONS

1 Place chicken in slow cooker. Cover with barbecue sauce. Cover; cook on LOW 8 to 9 hours.

2 Before serving, cut bacon slices in half. Cook bacon in microwave or on stove top, keeping bacon flat.

3 Place 2 slices cooked bacon over each piece of chicken in slow cooker. Top with cheese slices. Turn slow cooker to HIGH. Cover; cook on HIGH until cheese melts.

....

NOTE

If the sauce becomes too thick during cooking, add a little water.

ORANGE GINGER SALMON
MAKES 4 SERVINGS

1 salmon fillet (about 2 pounds)
Salt and black pepper

½ cup sesame-ginger salad dressing

2 navel oranges, peeled and sectioned

1 Preheat oven to 400°F. Line baking sheet with foil.

2 Place salmon fillet on prepared baking sheet; sprinkle with salt and pepper. Bake about 20 minutes or until salmon just begins to flake when tested with fork.

3 Meanwhile, bring dressing to a boil in small saucepan over medium heat; continue boiling until sauce is reduced by about half.

4 Top salmon with orange segments. Spoon sauce over top. Bake another 2 to 3 minutes or until heated through. Transfer salmon to serving platter; spoon sauce over top.

CHICKEN WITH HERB STUFFING
MAKES 4 SERVINGS

⅓ cup fresh basil leaves

1 package (8 ounces) goat cheese with garlic and herbs

4 boneless skinless chicken breasts

1 to 2 tablespoons olive oil

1 Place basil in food processor; process using on/off pulsing action until chopped. Cut goat cheese into large pieces and add to food processor; process using on/off pulsing action until combined.

2 Preheat oven to 350°F. Place 1 chicken breast on cutting board and cover with plastic wrap. Pound with meat mallet until ¼ inch thick. Repeat with remaining chicken.

3 Shape about 2 tablespoons of cheese mixture into log and set in center of each chicken breast. Wrap chicken around filling to enclose completely. Tie securely with kitchen string.

4 Heat 1 tablespoon oil in large ovenproof skillet; brown chicken bundles on all sides, adding additional oil as needed to prevent sticking. Place skillet in oven; bake 15 minutes or until chicken is cooked through and filling is hot. Allow to cool slightly, remove string and slice to serve.

SHELLS AND GORGONZOLA
MAKES 4 TO 6 SERVINGS

1 **pound uncooked medium shell pasta**

1 **jar (24 ounces) vodka sauce**

1 **package (4 ounces) crumbled gorgonzola cheese**

....

1 Cook pasta according to package directions. Drain well; cover and keep warm.

2 Meanwhile, heat sauce in medium saucepan over medium heat.

3 Toss pasta with sauce until well blended. Stir in cheese just before serving.

....

VARIATION

Add 2 cups packed torn spinach to hot drained pasta; stir
hot sauce into pasta and spinach. Stir in cheese and sprinkle
with chopped fresh rosemary just before serving.

TUNA PIES
MAKES 4 SERVINGS

1 can (8 ounces) refrigerated crescent roll dough

1 can (about 5 ounces) water-packed tuna, drained

1 tablespoon mayonnaise

1 cup (4 ounces) shredded Cheddar cheese

1 Preheat oven to 400°F. Separate crescent dough into triangles; press two perforated triangles together to form four rectangles. Press rectangles into bottoms and up sides of four ovenproof mugs or ramekins.

2 Combine tuna and mayonnaise in small bowl; mix gently. Spoon tuna mixture evenly over dough; sprinkle with cheese.

3 Bake 10 minutes or until dough is golden brown. Let cool slightly before serving.

VARIATION

You can add your favorite vegetables, like broccoli or peas, to this recipe, as well as trying other types of cheese, like mozzarella or Swiss.

KALUA PIG
MAKES 6 SERVINGS

3 slices bacon
1½ tablespoons coarse sea salt

1 boneless pork shoulder roast
   (5 to 6 pounds)
1 tablespoon liquid smoke

SLOW COOKER DIRECTIONS

1 Line slow cooker with bacon. Rub salt generously over pork; place on top of bacon. Pour liquid smoke over pork.

2 Cover; cook on LOW 16 to 18 hours. Remove pork to large cutting board; shred with two forks. *Do not shred pork in cooking liquid.*

SERVING SUGGESTIONS

Serve with hot cooked white rice topped
with sliced green onion and chopped fresh cilantro,
cabbage and/or fresh pineapple wedges.

NOTE

To shred pork, face two forks back
to back, pull forks in opposite directions
breaking up meat as you pull.

HONEY-ROASTED CHICKEN AND BUTTERNUT SQUASH
MAKES 4 TO 6 SERVINGS

1 pound fresh butternut squash chunks

Salt and black pepper

6 bone-in chicken thighs

1 tablespoon honey

1 Preheat oven to 375°F. Spray baking sheet and wire rack with nonstick cooking spray.

2 Spread squash on prepared baking sheet; season with salt and pepper.

3 Place wire rack over squash; place chicken on rack. Season with salt and pepper.

4 Roast 25 minutes. Carefully lift rack and stir squash; brush honey over chicken pieces. Roast 20 minutes or until chicken is cooked through (165°F).

POSOLE
MAKES 8 SERVINGS

3 pounds pork tenderloin, cubed

3 cans (about 14 ounces each) white hominy, drained

¾ cup chili sauce

SLOW COOKER DIRECTIONS

Combine pork, hominy and chili sauce in slow cooker. Cover; cook on LOW 10 hours or on HIGH 5 hours.

HONEY-ROASTED CHICKEN AND BUTTERNUT SQUASH

GRILLED YOUNG TURKEY
MAKES 8 SERVINGS

1 (4½- to 9-pound) young turkey, thawed if frozen, giblets removed

Vegetable oil

....

1 Prepare grill for indirect cooking over medium heat. Rub oil over grill grid to prevent sticking.

2 Turn wings back to hold neck skin in place. Tie legs with kitchen string to maintain tucked position. Brush entire turkey with oil to prevent skin from drying. Insert meat thermometer into thickest part of thigh not touching bone.

3 Place unstuffed turkey, breast up, in center of grill grid over drip pan. Cover grill; leave vents open. If using charcoal grill, add 6 to 8 briquettes to each side every hour or as needed to maintain heat. Cook turkey to internal thigh temperature of 180°F and breast to 170°F. (Begin checking smaller turkey at about 1½ hours; 9-pound turkey may take up to 2½ hours for doneness.)

....

NOTE
To set up gas grill for indirect cooking, preheat all burners on high. Turn one burner off; place food over "off" burner. Reset remaining burner(s) to medium. Close lid to cook. To set up charcoal grill for indirect cooking, arrange hot coals around outer edge of grill; place disposable aluminum pan in open space. Place food over open area, and close lid to cook.

BAKED HAM WITH SWEET AND SPICY GLAZE
MAKES 8 TO 10 SERVINGS

1 (8-pound) bone-in smoked half ham

Sweet and Spicy Glaze (recipe follows)

1 Preheat oven to 325°F. Place ham, fat side up, in roasting pan. Bake 3 hours.

2 Prepare Sweet and Spicy Glaze. Remove ham from oven. Generously brush half of glaze over ham; bake 30 minutes or until thermometer inserted into thickest part of ham registers 160°F.

3 Remove ham from oven; brush with remaining glaze. Let stand about 20 minutes before slicing.

SWEET AND SPICY GLAZE
MAKES ABOUT 2 CUPS

¾ cup packed brown sugar

⅓ cup cider vinegar

¼ cup golden raisins

1 can (8¾ ounces) sliced peaches in heavy syrup, drained, chopped and syrup reserved

1 tablespoon cornstarch

¼ cup orange juice

1 can (8¼ ounces) crushed pineapple in syrup, undrained

1 tablespoon grated orange peel

1 clove garlic, minced

½ teaspoon red pepper flakes

½ teaspoon grated fresh ginger

1 Combine brown sugar, vinegar, raisins and peach syrup in medium saucepan. Bring to a boil over high heat. Reduce heat to low; simmer 8 to 10 minutes.

2 Whisk cornstarch into orange juice in small bowl until smooth and well blended. Stir into brown sugar mixture. Stir peaches, pineapple, orange peel, garlic, red pepper flakes and ginger into saucepan; bring to a boil over medium heat. Cook until sauce is thickened, stirring constantly.

QUICK & EASY CHICKEN PESTO SALAD
MAKES 2 SERVINGS

1 package (3 ounces) ramen noodles, any flavor, broken into 4 large chunks*

1 cup chopped cooked chicken

½ cup halved grape tomatoes

¼ cup slivered or finely chopped carrots

1 to 2 tablespoons prepared pesto

Salt and black pepper

Discard seasoning packet.

1 Prepare noodles according to package directions. Rinse and drain under cool running water.

2 Combine noodles, chicken, tomatoes, carrots and pesto in large bowl; toss to coat. Season with salt and pepper.

GLAZED PORK LOIN
MAKES 4 SERVINGS

1 bag (1 pound) baby carrots

4 boneless pork loin chops

1 jar (8 ounces) apricot preserves

SLOW COOKER DIRECTIONS

1 Place carrots in slow cooker. Place pork on carrots; spread with preserves.

2 Cover; cook on LOW 8 hours or on HIGH 4 hours.

SERVING SUGGESTION

Serve with seasoned or cheese-flavored mashed potatoes.

QUICK & EASY CHICKEN PESTO SALAD

CRISPY RANCH CHICKEN BITES

MAKES 4 SERVINGS

1 **pound boneless skinless chicken breasts**

¾ **cup ranch dressing, plus additional for serving**

2 **cups panko bread crumbs**

1 Preheat oven to 375°F. Line baking sheet with foil; spray foil with nonstick cooking spray.

2 Cut chicken into 1-inch cubes. Place ¾ cup ranch dressing in small bowl. Spread panko in shallow dish. Dip chicken in ranch dressing; shake off excess. Roll in panko to coat. Place breaded chicken on prepared baking sheet. Spray with cooking spray.

3 Bake 15 to 17 minutes or until golden brown and cooked through, turning once. Serve with additional ranch dressing.

GLAZED CORNED BEEF
MAKES 6 TO 8 SERVINGS

1 corned beef brisket (about 2 pounds), rinsed

¾ cup apricot jam

2 tablespoons packed brown sugar

½ teaspoon ground red pepper

1 Preheat oven to 350°F. Place corned beef in roasting pan. Cover with foil. Bake 45 minutes.

2 Combine jam, brown sugar and red pepper in small bowl. Reserve half of jam mixture; set aside. Uncover corned beef; brush with 2 tablespoons of jam mixture. Roast 20 minutes; brush with another 2 tablespoons jam mixture. Roast additional 20 minutes or until glazed.

3 Cut into thin slices to serve. Serve with reserved jam mixture.

HOT & SOUR CHICKEN
MAKES 4 TO 6 SERVINGS

4 to 6 boneless skinless chicken breasts (about 1 to 1½ pounds)

1 cup chicken or vegetable broth

1 package (1 ounce) dry hot-and-sour soup mix

Steamed sugar snap peas and diced red bell pepper (optional)

SLOW COOKER DIRECTIONS

1 Place chicken in slow cooker. Add broth and dry soup mix.

2 Cover; cook on LOW 5 to 6 hours. Serve over peas and bell pepper, if desired.

GLAZED CORNED BEEF

STIR-FRY CUPS

MAKES 6 CUPS

1 package (10 ounces) frozen puff pastry shells

1 bag (21 ounces) frozen vegetable stir-fry mix with teriyaki sauce

1 package (6 ounces) cooked diced chicken breast

....

1 Bake pastry shells according to package directions.

2 Meanwhile, prepare stir-fry mix according to package directions. Add chicken; cook and stir until heated through.

3 Spoon stir-fry mixture into prepared pastry shells, allowing some of the mixture to spill over the side.

....

VARIATION

To make this meal even simpler, use chicken stir-fry mix. Sprinkle sliced almonds on top to dress it up and add flavor.

QUICK-BRAISED CHICKEN THIGHS & VEGETABLES
MAKES 4 SERVINGS

2 tablespoons all-purpose flour

1 teaspoon dried thyme

½ teaspoon salt

¼ teaspoon black pepper

4 large bone-in chicken thighs (1½ to 1¾ pounds), skin removed

2 teaspoons olive oil

1 cup chicken broth

12 ounces fresh green beans, trimmed and cut into 1-inch pieces

1 large red bell pepper, cut into short, thin strips

¼ cup grated Parmesan cheese

1 Combine flour, thyme, salt and black pepper in large resealable food storage bag. Add chicken, one piece at a time; shake to coat lightly with flour mixture.

2 Heat oil in large deep skillet over medium heat until hot. Place chicken meat sides down in skillet; sprinkle any remaining flour mixture from bag over chicken. Cook 5 minutes; turn chicken over, add broth to skillet. Simmer, uncovered, 15 minutes, turning once.

3 Add green beans and bell pepper to skillet. Cover; simmer 8 to 10 minutes or until vegetables are tender and chicken is cooked through and juices run clear. Transfer chicken to serving plates. Stir vegetable mixture; serve vegetables over chicken. Sprinkle with Parmesan cheese.

BACON AND ONION BRISKET
MAKES 6 SERVINGS

6 slices bacon, cut crosswise into ½-inch strips

1 flat-cut boneless beef brisket, seasoned with salt and black pepper (about 2½ pounds)

3 medium onions, sliced

2 cans (10½ ounces each) condensed beef consommé, undiluted

SLOW COOKER DIRECTIONS

1 Cook bacon in large skillet over medium-high heat about 3 minutes. *Do not overcook.* Transfer bacon with slotted spoon to 5-quart slow cooker.

2 Sear brisket in hot bacon drippings on all sides, turning as it browns. Transfer to slow cooker.

3 Lower skillet heat to medium. Add sliced onions to skillet. Cook and stir 3 to 5 minutes or until softened. Add to slow cooker. Pour in consommé. Cover; cook on HIGH 6 to 8 hours or until meat is tender.

4 Transfer brisket to cutting board and let rest 10 minutes. Slice brisket against the grain into thin slices, and arrange on platter. Season with salt and pepper, if desired. Spoon bacon, onions and cooking liquid over brisket to serve.

GLAZED HOLIDAY HAM
MAKES 24 SERVINGS

1 (6- to 7-pound) 30%-less-sodium, smoked, fully cooked, bone-in, spiral-cut ham half

½ cup cranberry chutney* or raspberry or apricot preserves

2 tablespoons horseradish mustard or Dijon-style mustard

Look for cranberry chutney in the condiment section of your supermarket.

1 Preheat oven to 350°F.

2 Place ham on rack of broiler pan. Cover with foil. Bake 1½ to 2 hours or until internal temperature reaches 120°F.

3 Combine chutney and mustard in small bowl; mix well. Remove ham from oven. Discard foil. Spread chutney mixture evenly over surface of ham. Return to oven. Bake, uncovered, 30 minutes or until internal temperature reaches 140°F.

4 Let stand 5 minutes before slicing.

COOK'S NOTE
Leftovers keep up to 1 week in the refrigerator.

FAJITA-SEASONED GRILLED CHICKEN
MAKES 2 SERVINGS

2 boneless skinless chicken breasts (about 4 ounces each)

1 bunch green onions, ends trimmed

1 tablespoon olive oil

2 teaspoons fajita seasoning mix

1 Prepare grill for direct cooking.

2 Brush chicken and green onions with oil. Sprinkle both sides of chicken breasts with seasoning mix. Grill chicken and green onions 6 to 8 minutes or until chicken is no longer pink in center.

3 Serve chicken with green onions.

SPICY SHREDDED CHICKEN
MAKES 6 SERVINGS

6 boneless skinless chicken breasts (about 1½ pounds)

1 jar (16 ounces) salsa

Flour tortillas (optional)

SLOW COOKER DIRECTIONS

Place chicken in slow cooker. Cover with salsa. Cover; cook on LOW 6 to 8 hours or until chicken is tender and no longer pink in center. Shred chicken with two forks; serve in tortillas, if desired.

NOTE

To shred chicken, face two forks back to back, pull forks in opposite directions breaking up meat as you pull.

FAJITA-SEASONED GRILLED CHICKEN

QUICK PASTA PUTTANESCA
MAKES 6 TO 8 SERVINGS

1 package (16 ounces) uncooked spaghetti or linguine

3 tablespoons plus 1 teaspoon olive oil, divided

¼ to 1 teaspoon red pepper flakes*

1 tablespoon dried minced onion

1 teaspoon minced garlic

2 cans (about 6 ounces each) chunk light tuna packed in water, drained

1 can (28 ounces) diced tomatoes

1 can (8 ounces) tomato sauce

24 pitted kalamata or black olives

2 tablespoons capers, drained

For a mildly spicy dish, use ¼ teaspoon red pepper flakes. For a very spicy dish, use 1 teaspoon red pepper flakes.

1 Cook spaghetti according to package directions; drain and return to saucepan. Add 1 teaspoon oil; toss to coat. Cover and keep warm.

2 Heat remaining 3 tablespoons oil in large skillet over medium-high heat. Add red pepper flakes; cook and stir until sizzling. Add onion and garlic; cook and stir 1 minute. Add tuna; cook and stir 2 to 3 minutes. Add tomatoes, tomato sauce, olives and capers; cook until sauce is heated through, stirring frequently.

3 Add sauce to pasta; stir until coated. Serve immediately.

NEW YORK STRIP STEAKS WITH WILD MUSHROOM SAUCE
MAKES 4 SERVINGS

4 New York strip steaks (about 6 ounces each)

Wild Mushroom Sauce (recipe follows)

Broil or grill steaks 5 to 6 minutes per side or until desired doneness. Prepare and serve with Wild Mushroom Sauce.

WILD MUSHROOM SAUCE
MAKES 3 CUPS

3 tablespoons olive oil

8 ounces assorted wild mushrooms, sliced

8 ounces button mushrooms, sliced

1½ teaspoons minced fresh basil

1½ teaspoons minced fresh thyme

3 cups beef broth, divided

1½ cups sliced green onions

1½ tablespoons cornstarch

2 tablespoons minced fresh parsley

Salt and hot pepper sauce

1 Heat oil in large skillet over medium heat. Add mushrooms, basil and thyme; cook and stir 5 minutes or until mushrooms release their liquid. Cook 10 minutes, stirring occasionally, until mushrooms are browned and all liquid is evaporated.

2 Add 2¾ cups broth and green onions; bring to a boil. Reduce heat; simmer, uncovered, 10 to 12 minutes or until broth is reduced by one third.

3 Combine cornstarch and remaining ¼ cup broth in small cup. Add to mushroom mixture. Boil, stirring constantly, 1 to 2 minutes or until thickened. Stir in parsley. Season with salt and hot pepper sauce.

MAC AND CHEESE TOSS

MAKES 4 SERVINGS

8 ounces ham, diced

4 cups (1 quart) prepared deli
macaroni and cheese

½ cup frozen green peas, thawed

¼ cup milk

MICROWAVE DIRECTIONS

1 Combine all ingredients in microwavable 2-quart casserole. Toss gently to blend.

2 Microwave, covered, on HIGH 3 minutes; stir. Microwave 1 minute or until heated through.

NOTE

To thaw peas quickly, place them in a small
colander under cold running water 15 to 20 seconds
or until thawed. Drain liquid.

CRISPY MUSTARD CHICKEN
MAKES 4 SERVINGS

4 bone-in chicken breasts
Salt and black pepper
⅓ cup Dijon mustard

½ cup panko bread crumbs or coarse dry bread crumbs

1 Preheat oven to 350°F. Spray rack of broiler pan or shallow baking pan with nonstick cooking spray.

2 Remove skin from chicken. Season chicken with salt and pepper; place on prepared rack. Bake 20 minutes.

3 Brush chicken generously with mustard. Sprinkle with panko and gently press panko into mustard. Bake 20 to 25 minutes or until chicken is cooked through (165°F).

SHRIMP PARMESAN
MAKES 4 SERVINGS

1 package (16 ounces) frozen breaded shrimp
1 cup pasta sauce

1 cup (4 ounces) shredded Italian cheese blend

1 Preheat oven to 450°F. Spread shrimp on baking sheet in single layer. Bake 10 minutes, turning once.

2 Transfer shrimp to 11×7-inch baking dish. Top shrimp with dollops of sauce; sprinkle with cheese.

3 Bake 5 minutes or until sauce is heated and cheese is melted.

CRISPY MUSTARD CHICKEN

TUSCAN PASTA
MAKES 6 SERVINGS

12 ounces uncooked rigatoni or any shaped pasta

Tuscan Tomato Sauce (recipe follows)

⅓ cup grated Parmesan cheese, or to taste

1 Cook pasta according to package directions until al dente. Drain well; cover and keep warm.

2 Prepare Tuscan Tomato Sauce. Serve sauce over pasta. Sprinkle with cheese.

TUSCAN TOMATO SAUCE
MAKES 3 CUPS

2 tablespoons olive oil

½ cup chopped onion

2 cloves garlic, minced

8 plum tomatoes, coarsely chopped

1 can (8 ounces) tomato sauce

1 teaspoon *each* chopped fresh basil, oregano and rosemary leaves

½ teaspoon salt

½ teaspoon black pepper

1 Heat oil in medium saucepan over medium heat. Add onion; cook and stir 4 minutes or until tender. Add garlic; cook 1 minute.

2 Stir in tomatoes, tomato sauce, herbs, salt and pepper; bring to a boil. Reduce heat; simmer, uncovered, 6 minutes or until desired consistency is reached, stirring occasionally.

FAVORITE GREEN BEANS
MAKES 6 SERVINGS

1 pound green beans (ends trimmed)

2 tablespoons margarine

¼ cup grated Parmesan cheese

1 teaspoon garlic salt

1 Bring 1 quart of water to a boil in large saucepan. Add green beans and boil 3 minutes. Remove from heat and drain.

2 Heat margarine in large skillet over medium heat. Add green beans to skillet and top with Parmesan cheese and garlic salt. Cook 5 minutes, stirring occasionally. Remove from heat and serve warm.

SMASHED POTATOES
MAKES 4 SERVINGS

4 medium russet potatoes (about 1½ pounds), peeled and cut into ¼-inch cubes

⅓ cup milk

2 tablespoons sour cream

1 tablespoon minced onion

½ teaspoon salt

¼ teaspoon black pepper

⅛ teaspoon garlic powder (optional)

Chopped fresh chives or French fried onions (optional)

....

1 Bring large saucepan of lightly salted water to a boil. Add potatoes; cook 15 to 20 minutes or until fork-tender. Drain and return to saucepan.

2 Slightly mash potatoes. Stir in milk, sour cream, minced onion, salt, pepper and garlic powder, if desired. Mash until desired texture is reached, leaving potatoes chunky. Cook 5 minutes over low heat or until heated through, stirring occasionally. Top with chives, if desired.

SUPER SIMPLE CHEESY BUBBLE LOAF
MAKES 12 SERVINGS

2 packages (12 ounces each) refrigerated buttermilk biscuits (10 biscuits per package)

2 tablespoons butter, melted

1½ cups (6 ounces) shredded Italian cheese blend

....

1 Preheat oven to 350°F. Spray 9×5-inch loaf pan with nonstick cooking spray.

2 Separate biscuits; cut each biscuit into four pieces with scissors. Layer half of biscuit pieces in prepared pan. Drizzle with 1 tablespoon butter; sprinkle with 1 cup cheese. Top with remaining biscuit pieces, 1 tablespoon butter and ½ cup cheese.

3 Bake about 25 minutes or until golden brown. Serve warm.

....

TIP
It's easy to change up the flavors in this simple bread.
Try Mexican cheese blend instead of Italian, and add taco seasoning mix and/or hot pepper sauce to the melted butter before drizzling it over the dough. Or, sprinkle ¼ cup chopped ham, salami or crumbled crisp-cooked bacon between the layers of dough.

BROCCOLI WITH CHEESE SAUCE
MAKES 3 TO 4 SERVINGS

12 ounces fresh broccoli, cut into spears with 2- or 3-inch stems

8 ounces pasteurized process cheese product, cubed

3 tablespoons milk

½ teaspoon Worcestershire sauce

....

MICROWAVE DIRECTIONS

1 Arrange broccoli spears on microwavable dinner plate with stalks toward outside of plate; cover with vented plastic wrap. Microwave on HIGH 3 to 4 minutes or until broccoli stems are tender.

2 Combine cheese product, milk and Worcestershire sauce in 2-quart glass measuring cup. Microwave on HIGH 2 minutes; stir. If cheese product is not completely melted, microwave 1 minute more, stirring after 30 seconds, until melted. Serve sauce over broccoli.

MASHED POTATO PUFFS
MAKES 18 PUFFS (ABOUT 6 SERVINGS)

1 cup prepared mashed potatoes
½ cup finely chopped broccoli or spinach

2 egg whites
4 tablespoons shredded Parmesan cheese, divided

1 Preheat oven to 400°F. Spray 18 mini (1¾-inch) muffin cups with nonstick cooking spray.

2 Combine mashed potatoes, broccoli, egg whites and 2 tablespoons Parmesan cheese in large bowl; mix well. Spoon evenly into prepared muffin cups. Sprinkle with remaining 2 tablespoons Parmesan cheese.

3 Bake 20 to 23 minutes or until golden brown. To remove from pan, gently run knife around outer edges and lift out with fork. Serve warm.

BROCCOLI SUPREME
MAKES 7 SERVINGS

2 packages (10 ounces each) frozen chopped broccoli

1 cup chicken or vegetable broth

2 tablespoons mayonnaise

2 teaspoons dried minced onion (optional)

1 Combine broccoli, broth, mayonnaise and onion, if desired, in large saucepan. Cover and simmer over medium heat until broccoli is tender, stirring occasionally.

2 Uncover; continue to simmer until liquid has evaporated, stirring occasionally.

SUGAR-AND-SPICE TWISTS
MAKES 12 SERVINGS

2 tablespoons granulated sugar
½ teaspoon ground cinnamon

1 package (11 ounces) refrigerated breadstick dough (12 breadsticks)

1 Preheat oven to 350°F. Line baking sheet with parchment paper or spray with nonstick cooking spray.

2 Combine sugar and cinnamon in shallow dish or plate. Separate breadsticks; roll each piece into 12-inch rope. Roll ropes in sugar-cinnamon mixture to coat. Twist each rope into pretzel shape. Place on prepared baking sheet.

3 Bake 15 to 18 minutes or until lightly browned. Remove to wire rack to cool 5 minutes. Serve warm.

HINT

Use colored sugar sprinkles in place of the granulated sugar in this recipe for a fun "twist" of color perfect for holidays, birthdays or simple everyday celebrations.

GREEK PASTA SALAD

MAKES 6 SERVINGS

SALAD

6 cups cooked regular, tri-color or multigrain rotini pasta

1½ cups sliced zucchini

1 cup diced red bell pepper (about 1 medium)

12 medium pitted black olives (optional)

¼ cup chopped fresh dill (optional)

1 package (4 ounces) crumbled feta cheese

DRESSING

¼ cup olive oil

¼ cup lemon juice

¼ teaspoon salt

¼ teaspoon dried oregano

⅛ teaspoon black pepper

1 For pasta salad, combine pasta, zucchini, bell pepper, olives and dill, if desired, in large bowl; toss to blend.

2 For dressing, combine oil, lemon juice, salt, oregano and black pepper in small bowl; stir to blend. Pour over pasta; toss to coat.

3 Just before serving, top with feta cheese.

MASHED CAULIFLOWER
MAKES 6 SERVINGS

2 heads cauliflower (to equal
  8 cups florets)

1 tablespoon butter or as needed

1 tablespoon half-and-half or
  whipping cream

Salt

1 Break cauliflower into equal-size florets. Place in large saucepan in about 2 inches of water. Simmer over medium heat 20 to 25 minutes or until cauliflower is very tender and falling apart. (Check occasionally to make sure there is enough water to prevent burning; add water if necessary.) Drain well.

2 Place cooked cauliflower in food processor or blender. Process until almost smooth. Add butter. Process until smooth, adding half-and-half as needed to reach desired consistency. Season with salt to taste.

QUICK BANANA SPLIT SHORTCAKE
MAKES 6 SERVINGS

1 (14-ounce) pound cake or marble cake

6 small bananas

1 quart Neapolitan ice cream

....

1 Slice cake into 12 slices. Place one slice on each side of six dessert bowls.

2 Slice bananas and sprinkle evenly over cake.

3 Top dessert with equal amounts ice cream.

....

EXTRAS
For an extra decadent dessert, heat the cake and bananas in microwavable bowls for 15 seconds or until warm. Top with ice cream and marshmallow topping or caramel sauce.

CANDY CALZONES
MAKES 16 CALZONES

1 package small chocolate, peanut and nougat candy bars, chocolate peanut butter cups or other chocolate candy bar (8 bars)

1 package (about 15 ounces) refrigerated pie crusts (2 crusts)

½ cup milk chocolate chips

....

1 Preheat oven to 375°F. Line baking sheet with parchment paper. Chop candy into ¼-inch pieces.

2 Unroll pie crusts on cutting board or clean work surface. Cut out 3-inch circles with biscuit cutter. Place about 1 tablespoon chopped candy on one side of each circle; fold dough over candy to form semicircle. Crimp edges with fingers or fork to seal. Place on prepared baking sheet.

3 Bake about 12 minutes or until crust is golden brown. Remove to wire rack to cool slightly.

4 Place chocolate chips in small microwavable bowl; microwave on HIGH 1 minute. Stir; microwave in 30-second intervals, stirring in between, until smooth. Drizzle melted chocolate over calzones; serve warm.

COFFEE TOFFEE ICE CREAM SANDWICHES
MAKES 4 SANDWICHES

1 **cup coffee ice cream**
¼ **cup milk chocolate toffee bits**

8 **vanilla pizzelles**

....

1 Let ice cream stand at room temperature 10 minutes or until slightly softened. Place toffee bits in shallow dish.

2 Carefully spread ¼ cup ice cream over one pizzelle. Top with second pizzelle; press together lightly. Roll edge in toffee bits. Repeat with remaining ingredients. Wrap each sandwich in plastic wrap; freeze overnight or until firm.

....

TIP
You can substitute one toffee candy bar, crushed
into pieces, for the toffee baking bits.

QUICK CINNAMON APPLE BAKE
MAKES 1 SERVING

1 small apple, coarsely chopped

1 teaspoon packed brown sugar

½ teaspoon vanilla

¼ teaspoon ground cinnamon

1 teaspoon fresh lemon juice

1 tablespoon old-fashioned oats

1 teaspoon raisins or dried cranberries

1 teaspoon finely chopped walnuts or pecans

1 teaspoon butter or margarine

Vanilla ice cream (optional)

MICROWAVE DIRECTIONS

1 Combine apple, brown sugar, vanilla and cinnamon in small microwavable dish or mug; gently toss to coat. Sprinkle with lemon juice. Top evenly with oats, raisins and walnuts. Dot with butter.

2 Microwave on HIGH 2 minutes or until apples are tender. Let stand 1 to 2 minutes before serving. Top with ice cream, if desired.

MY OWN BERRY PIE
MAKES 3 SERVINGS

1 refrigerated pie crust (half of 15-ounce package)

2 cups fresh or frozen blueberries

2 tablespoons sugar, plus additional for topping

2 tablespoons all-purpose flour

1 teaspoon lemon peel

¼ teaspoon vanilla

¼ teaspoon ground cinnamon

1 tablespoon butter, cut into small pieces

1 egg

1 teaspoon water

1 Preheat oven to 375°F. Spray three ovenproof jars, mugs or ramekins with nonstick cooking spray.

2 Cut pie crust into six equal pieces. Press one piece into bottom of each prepared jar.

3 Combine blueberries, 2 tablespoons sugar, flour, lemon peel, vanilla and cinnamon in medium bowl; toss gently to coat. Spoon mixture over crusts in jars; dot with butter.

4 Cut remaining three pieces of dough into ½-inch strips. Arrange strips in lattice design over top of each jar; press ends of strips securely to seal. Beat egg and water in small bowl; brush over lattice. Sprinkle with additional sugar. Place jars on baking sheet.

5 Bake 40 to 45 minutes or until crusts are golden brown. Let stand 10 to 15 minutes before serving.

S'MORE MONKEY BREAD
MAKES 5 SERVINGS

¼ cup graham cracker crumbs
¼ cup packed brown sugar
2 tablespoons butter, melted

1 package (7½ ounces) refrigerated buttermilk biscuits (10 biscuits)
¼ cup milk chocolate chips
¾ cup mini marshmallows

1 Preheat oven to 350°F. Spray five 4-ounce ramekins or custard cups with nonstick cooking spray.

2 Combine graham cracker crumbs and brown sugar in medium bowl. Place melted butter in small bowl.

3 Separate biscuits; cut each biscuit into four pieces with scissors. Dip four biscuit pieces in melted butter; roll in crumb mixture to coat. Place in prepared ramekin; sprinkle with about seven chocolate chips and seven marshmallows, pressing chips into biscuit dough. Dip four more biscuit pieces into melted butter; roll in crumb mixture to coat. Arrange pieces over bottom layer in ramekin; top with chocolate chips and marshmallows. Repeat with remaining ingredients and ramekins. Place ramekins on baking sheet.

4 Bake about 18 minutes or until golden brown. Serve warm.

VARIATION

To use a muffin pan instead of ramekins, double all ingredients. Spray 11 standard (2½-inch) muffin pan cups with nonstick cooking spray. Use seven biscuit pieces in each muffin cup, layering with chocolate chips and mini marshmallows as directed in step 3. Bake as directed above. Loosen edges of muffins with knife immediately after baking; remove muffins to serving plate. Makes 11 muffins.

APPLES WITH BROWN SUGAR AND CINNAMON

MAKES 4 SERVINGS

2 tablespoons packed brown sugar

1 tablespoon ground cinnamon

¼ teaspoon ground nutmeg

2 large apples (Red Delicious, Braeburn or Fuji), cored and sliced into 12 rings

Caramel or butterscotch sauce, warmed

Vanilla ice cream (optional)

1 Combine brown sugar, cinnamon and nutmeg in small bowl. Spray 8- or 9-inch baking dish with nonstick cooking spray. Place apples in large bowl.

2 Preheat oven to 350°F.

3 Sprinkle apples with brown sugar mixture. Layer apple slices in baking dish, overlapping as necessary. Cook 25 to 30 minutes or until tender, turning as needed, until rich brown, but not mushy.

4 Place on four plates and drizzle with caramel sauce. Add ice cream, if desired.

NOTE

You can also grill apples, if you like. Wrap apple slices in foil, grill over medium-low heat for about 9 minutes. Other fruit, like peaches and nectarines, also work great, too!

BROWNIE BOTTOM ICE CREAM PIE
MAKES 8 SERVINGS

1 package (about 16 ounces)
   refrigerated brownie batter

5 to 6 cups fudge ripple, cookies
   and cream or favorite flavor
   ice cream, softened

1 jar (8 ounces) hot fudge
   topping

....

1 Preheat oven to 350°F. Spray 9-inch pie pan with nonstick cooking spray. Let batter stand at room temperature 5 minutes to soften.

2 Place batter in prepared pan; use dampened hands to spread batter over bottom and halfway up side of pan. Bake about 20 minutes or until toothpick inserted into center comes out clean. Cool completely in pan on wire rack.

3 Top brownie layer with ice cream, spreading to edge of pie pan. Serve immediately or cover with plastic wrap and freeze up to several hours. (If frozen, let pie stand at room temperature 10 minutes to soften.) Drizzle with hot fudge topping before serving.

....

EXTRAS
Serve the pie with additional toppings such as
whipped cream, chopped nuts, sprinkles
and maraschino cherries.

PEACH MELBA COBBLER
MAKES 8 SERVINGS

2 packages (16 ounces each) frozen sliced peaches, thawed and drained

2 cups fresh raspberries

½ cup sugar

¼ cup all-purpose flour

3 tablespoons butter, melted

½ teaspoon vanilla

¼ teaspoon ground nutmeg

1 refrigerated pie crust (half of 15-ounce package), at room temperature

1 egg white, beaten

Vanilla ice cream (optional)

1 Preheat oven to 375°F.

2 Combine peaches, raspberries, sugar, flour, butter, vanilla and nutmeg in large bowl; toss to coat. Spoon into 2-quart oval baking dish.

3 Unroll pie crust and place over fruit, pressing dough against edge of baking dish with fork. Run knife along edge of dish to remove excess dough. Brush with egg white. Cut three slits in crust to vent.

4 Bake 50 to 60 minutes or until crust is light golden brown. Remove to wire rack; let stand 15 minutes before serving. Serve warm with ice cream, if desired.

NOTE

For a darker, shinier crust, brush with an egg yolk beaten with 1 tablespoon water before baking instead of the egg white.

MAPLE WALNUT APPLE CRESCENT COBBLER
MAKES 8 SERVINGS

FILLING

6 Golden Delicious apples
(2½ pounds), peeled and
thinly sliced

⅓ cup maple syrup

2 tablespoons all-purpose flour

2 teaspoons vanilla

⅛ teaspoon ground nutmeg

TOPPING

1 package (8 ounces)
refrigerated crescent roll
dough

4 teaspoons butter, melted

¼ cup chopped walnuts

2 tablespoons packed brown
sugar

1 Preheat oven to 375°F. Place rack in center of oven. Spray 8-inch square baking dish with nonstick cooking spray.

2 Combine apples, maple syrup, flour, vanilla and nutmeg in medium bowl; toss to coat. Spoon into prepared baking dish. Bake 30 minutes or until apples are tender but still firm.

3 Meanwhile, divide dough into eight triangles; place on work surface. Brush each triangle with melted butter. Combine walnuts and brown sugar in small bowl; sprinkle over dough. Roll up each dough triangle to form crescent. Arrange crescents over warm apple mixture in two rows.

4 Bake 15 minutes. Cover loosely with foil; bake 30 minutes. Uncover; bake 3 minutes or until filling is thick and bubbly and crescent rolls are golden brown.

INDIVIDUAL FRUIT PIE
MAKES 2 SERVINGS

1 refrigerated pie crust (half of a 15-ounce package)

¼ cup cherry, apple or blueberry pie filling

2 tablespoons butter, melted

1 teaspoon sugar

....

1 Preheat oven to 425°F. Line baking sheet with parchment paper.

2 Cut pie crust into four pieces. Place two crusts on prepared baking sheet. Divide pie filling evenly among crusts. Top with second crust. Crimp edge of dough with a fork to seal completely. Brush crusts with butter. Sprinkle with sugar.

3 Bake 12 to 14 minutes or until light golden brown. Remove to wire rack. Serve warm.

PISTACHIO POKE CAKE
MAKES 12 TO 15 SERVINGS

1 package (about 15 ounces)
   white cake mix, plus
   ingredients to prepare mix

1 package (4-serving size)
   pistachio instant pudding
   and pie filling mix, plus
   ingredients to prepare mix

1 cup chopped pistachio nuts

1 Prepare and bake cake mix according to package directions for 13×9-inch pan.
  Cool completely.

2 Prepare pudding mix according to package directions. Poke holes in cake at
  ½-inch intervals with wooden skewer. Pour pudding over cake. Sprinkle with
  pistachios. Refrigerate 2 to 3 hours or until firm.

INDEX

METRIC CONVERSION CHART

VOLUME MEASUREMENTS (dry)

$^1\!/_8$ teaspoon = 0.5 mL
$^1\!/_4$ teaspoon = 1 mL
$^1\!/_2$ teaspoon = 2 mL
$^3\!/_4$ teaspoon = 4 mL
1 teaspoon = 5 mL
1 tablespoon = 15 mL
2 tablespoons = 30 mL
$^1\!/_4$ cup = 60 mL
$^1\!/_3$ cup = 75 mL
$^1\!/_2$ cup = 125 mL
$^2\!/_3$ cup = 150 mL
$^3\!/_4$ cup = 175 mL
1 cup = 250 mL
2 cups = 1 pint = 500 mL
3 cups = 750 mL
4 cups = 1 quart = 1 L

VOLUME MEASUREMENTS (fluid)

1 fluid ounce (2 tablespoons) = 30 mL
4 fluid ounces ($^1\!/_2$ cup) = 125 mL
8 fluid ounces (1 cup) = 250 mL
12 fluid ounces (1$^1\!/_2$ cups) = 375 mL
16 fluid ounces (2 cups) = 500 mL

WEIGHTS (mass)

$^1\!/_2$ ounce = 15 g
1 ounce = 30 g
3 ounces = 90 g
4 ounces = 120 g
8 ounces = 225 g
10 ounces = 285 g
12 ounces = 360 g
16 ounces = 1 pound = 450 g

DIMENSIONS

$^1\!/_{16}$ inch = 2 mm
$^1\!/_8$ inch = 3 mm
$^1\!/_4$ inch = 6 mm
$^1\!/_2$ inch = 1.5 cm
$^3\!/_4$ inch = 2 cm
1 inch = 2.5 cm

OVEN TEMPERATURES

250°F = 120°C
275°F = 140°C
300°F = 150°C
325°F = 160°C
350°F = 180°C
375°F = 190°C
400°F = 200°C
425°F = 220°C
450°F = 230°C

BAKING PAN SIZES

Utensil	Size in Inches/Quarts	Metric Volume	Size in Centimeters
Baking or Cake Pan (square or rectangular)	8×8×2	2 L	20×20×5
	9×9×2	2.5 L	23×23×5
	12×8×2	3 L	30×20×5
	13×9×2	3.5 L	33×23×5
Loaf Pan	8×4×3	1.5 L	20×10×7
	9×5×3	2 L	23×13×7
Round Layer Cake Pan	8×1½	1.2 L	20×4
	9×1½	1.5 L	23×4
Pie Plate	8×1¼	750 mL	20×3
	9×1¼	1 L	23×3
Baking Dish or Casserole	1 quart	1 L	—
	1½ quart	1.5 L	—
	2 quart	2 L	—